SELECTED POEMS
of
MALCOLM LOWRY

SELECTED POEMS
of
MALCOLM LOWRY

Edited by
EARLE BIRNEY

with the assistance of
Margerie Lowry

City Lights Books | San Francisco

These poems have been selected and edited from manuscripts at the University of British Columbia. Some of them have already been published, or will appear, in: *Arizona Quarterly, Atlantic Monthly, Audience, Canadian Forum, Canadian Literature, Canadian Poetry Magazine, Contact, Contemporary Verse, Dalhousie Review, Evidence, Exchange, Fiddlehead, Harpers, Ladies Home Journal, London Magazine, Minnesota Review, New York Times, New Yorker, Northwest Review, Outposts, Paris Review, Perspective, Queens Quarterly, Southwest Review, Tamarack Review, Western Humanities Review, X*, and in A. J. M. Smith's *Book of Canadian Poetry*.

Library of Congress Cataloging-in-Publication Data
Names: Lowry, Malcolm, 1909-1957, author. | Birney, Earle, 1904–1995, editor.
Title: Selected poems of Malcolm Lowry / Malcolm Lowry ; edited by Earle Alfred Birney with the assistance of Margerie Lowry ; preface by Lawrence Ferlinghetti.
Description: San Francisco : City Lights Publishers, [2017] | Series: City lights pocket poets series ; 17
Identifiers: LCCN 2016041191 | ISBN 9780872867291 (paperback)
Subjects: | BISAC: POETRY / English, Irish, Scottish, Welsh.
Classification: LCC PR6023.O96 A6 2017 | DDC 821/.914—dc23
LC record available at https://lccn.loc.gov/2016041191

City Lights books are published at the City Lights Bookstore
261 Columbus Avenue, San Francisco, CA 94133
www.citylights.com

— June, too soon; July, stand by; August, you must; September, remember; October, all over.
                                            — Mariner's proverb

CONTENTS

I've never regretted taking ship to Vancouver B.C. and talking Earle Birney, keeper of Lowery's manuscripts, into giving me these poems to publish City Lights in 1962, though they were greeted with a loud silence in the world press.

I believe in the poems not a pure poetry but as the flawed record of a man, as Birney put it, "drowning in the lonely seas of alcohol and guilt." As such, he joins the company of great poets like Dylan Thomas who also drank and saw the spider.

—Lawrence Frelinghetti

Malcolm Lowry in front of his squatter's shack, Dollarton, British Columbia (circa 1953). Photo: David Markson.

'When the doomed are most eloquent in their *sinking*.' wrote Malcolm Lowry in one of the poems in this book, 'It seems that then we are least strong to save.' The words are the man; they have the wry, archaic irony of his talk, as it still sounds in my ears; they have his stance, teetering on a rope of comic fancies between grandeur and self-pity, between exultation in his own power and agonies of self-contempt. Even the image traces an epitaph; his whole life was a slow drowning in great lonely seas of alcohol and guilt. It was all one sea, and all his own. He sank in it a thousand times and struggled back up to reveal the creatures that swam round him under his glowing reefs and in his black abysses. His talk and his writing were endless and autistic in their compulsion and terror, but they carried an eloquence such as no other artist has ever shaped for such experience. And, for all that, he never phrased an exorcism to bring him back to land. Neither *Under the Volcano* nor the success of it, nor all the growing company of readers and friends, could save him from his destructive element.

He has dissolved into it now, leaving only the countenance, stricken yet curiously jovial, that haunts us from his writings. In the great novel, and in the stories of *Hear Us O Lord from Heaven Thy Dwelling Place*, and in those works still to be published we can see him through the naively translucent masks he put on. But here, in the poetry, we are confronted with the naked and doomed face of the man himself.

Who was he? An international man, surprise mutation born in 1909 into a family of wealthy Liverpool cottonbrokers;

fan of Beiderbecke and Voodoo, who suffered, in the inevitable British 'public school', as in his family, separateness and rejection; close reader of Marston and Melville, Nordahl Grieg and Hart Crane, toyer with the Kabbala and numerology, who took a classical tripos at Cambridge; teen-age weight lifter and guitar strummer who claimed Conrad Aiken as his spiritual father and wrote, while still an undergraduate, a novel under the influence of *Blue Voyage* fictionizing his seventeenth year, when he had knocked around the ports of Asia as a fireman's boy on a freighter; lover of outcasts and prisoners and seagulls, hater of patriots, evangelists, critics and other tenders of the mass mind. He married an American girl in Paris, took her to Cuernavaca, settling down to writing and tequila. After their divorce in 1939 he married a Hollywood starlet and writer, Margerie Bonner, now his widow. They came to British Columbia and moved into a tidal shack among a community of squatters along the Dollarton beach, in Vancouver's upper harbor. Apart from a few trips (Haiti, Rome, Paris), this was their home during his fourteen most productive years, 1940-54. From his beach went out the final revision of *Under the Volcano*, and most of the stories in *Hear Us O Lord* . . . Here also he wrote or re-wrote several hundred poems, in which he set down, without disguise, himself.

It was, I think, because his verse was so innocent of defenses, that he was chary of publishing it in his lifetime. With Margerie's help I pried a few out of him, in the year the *Volcano* appeared; they were published in some Canadian journals and anthologies, but remained unknown to his international following. Still he went on working seriously with poems, fitfully revising them between prodigious bouts not only of drinking but of sustained and sober prose writing, the pouring out of stories, novellas, novels, trilogies, plays, journals, letters, even film scripts.

Most of this lay unfinished, in disordered masses of manuscript, when Lowry choked to death in his sleep in a Sussex cottage, while on a visit to England in 1957. Eventually, it was brought back by Margerie to Vancouver and the University of British Columbia. Meantime an equally huge confusion of penciled scribblers and palimpsests of typing had been rescued by friends from his beach. While the Lowries were in Europe, their shack had been wrecked and burned into oblivion, along with the homes of all their fellow squatters, by the official preservers of Rent, Sanitation and Taxes. Margerie and I pooled the Dollarton manuscripts with the material from the English cottage, and began, a year ago, to edit the result. The first fruits of this collaboration are a novella. *Lunar Caustic*, appearing this year, and the present volume, A novel, *October Ferry to Gabriola*, as brilliant as anything Malcolm Lowry wrote, is next on the list for editing out of the great thicket of manuscript.

The present selection of poems contains about a fourth of those he completed. It has been chosen to represent the chief groupings which Lowry himself had made for a full edition he planned (under the title *The Lighthouse Invites the Storm*). Four of the subtitles used here were his own: The Roar of the Sea and the Darkness, The Cantinas, The Comedian, and Songs from the Beach: Eridanus. The order of the verses he had not fixed; the present one reflects roughly the chronology of his verse writing. The initial group is reminiscent in theme and sometimes in phrasing of that first novel, *Ultramarine*. The next two reflect the Mexican years, in the mid-Thirties. But all were re-worked, some many times, in the Dollarton beach shack, where most of the remainder were begun.

The bright crazy little shack is gone; all the sloppy ram-shackle honest pile houses where fishermen lived and kingfish-ers visited are bulldozed into limbo, along with the wild cherries and 'the forest path to the spring.' Now there is an empty beach and beside it a Park with picnic tables and tarmac access; the sea air stinks with car exhaust. And the city that ignored him plans to cement a bronze plaque in his memory to the brick wall of the new civic craphouse.

The world he could not live with is drowning in its own element. The self-drowned poet survives here in his.

— Earle Birney

Malcolm Lowry on the beach at Dollarton, British Columbia 1940–42. Photo: Earle Birney.

THE ROAR OF THE SEA
AND THE DARKNESS

NO KRAKEN SHALL BE FOUND TILL
SOUGHT BY NAME

Here is the ship, with decks all holy white,
Pure as the stone that scrubbed them to the bone.
Scuppers cleansed: and red lead shining where it
Would be, the blood all carefully washed from the deck,
The poop a pure arc on the Indian sky,
Cabined and perfect, with flag flying,
And bosun reading the bible, while with t'other hand
He gropes for Ahab's solution. And at the wheel
Another Ahab, whose rhetoric's however not his own.
Ah, who shall say that this is not the noblest of ships
Whose cargo's underwritten by heaven.
The dirt's all neatly hidden under winches,
The stokers are dropped overboard at night.
And sure her virtues do not lack acclaim
As, certain of salvage, she heads straight for the rocks
. . . Never so proud as in her hour of doom.

LOOK OUT! THE BLOODY BOSUN

A ship long laid up is a filthy thing
Cabled with rust, debris of the shore gang,
Filters gangrened, only a homesick tang
Reminds us of our longed-for suffering:
The sea ! The watches pass, the hours take wing
Like seagulls stuffed with bread. Tin-tin; pang-pang.
And this monotony is our *Sturm und Drang*
Of which few poets have the heart to sing.

I like to think we're scaling the old world
Down for a dose of red lead, as hammers snap
And ever grindstones wait to whet their lust.
Splendid to think so, yet in dreaming whirled
To abstract hulls, one falls into the trap
Set by that two-faced pimp who sees mere rust.

BYZANTIUM

— Don't come any of that Byzantium stuff
On me, me fine young toff! Just plain Stamboul
Is good enough for me and Lamps and Bill.
Constantibloodynople's right enough —
Used to be, eh? Eh? Don't give me that guff
Like that wot you said about the ideal
— In a blind eye socket! But a girl's a girl
And bobhead tigers here'll treat you rough,
And give you ideal! . . . I bid adieu,
The siren moos; oh whither where away,
The engine stampedes: more fool you, hee hee,
And ukuleles mourn a ululu,
The iron groans: every dog will have its day,
And stars wink: Venus first then Mercury.

OLD FREIGHTER IN AN OLD PORT

It had no name and we docked at midnight.
Nor could girls, shadowed at the dead car halt,
Laughing in linked quintets in the lamplight,
Leaven our hearts embittered with sea salt.
There was no beauty then about that place.
But waking early, to see near at hand
The wharf, road, and market, friendly clock face,
— The very lineaments of a new land —
Our flag run up the post office in spring,
Whose each stone seemed to promise news from one
Loved, and from our rusted bow the soaring
Car lines burning straight-ruled into the sun —
Emergence was of Christian from Despond
And Friday's print for Crusoe in the sand.

IRON CITIES

Iron thoughts sail out at evening on iron ships;
They move hushed as far lights while twelve footers
Dive at anchor as the ferry sputters
And spins like a round top, in the tide rips,
Its rooster voice half muted by choked pipes
Plumed with steam. The ship passes. The cutters
Fall away. Bells strike. The ferry utters
A last white phrase; and human lips
A last black one, heavy with welcome
To loss. Thoughts leave the pitiless city;
Yet ships themselves are iron and have no pity;
While men have hearts and sides that strain and rust.
Iron thoughts sail from the iron cities in the dust,
Yet soft as doves the thoughts that fly back home.

THE FLOWERING PAST

There is no poetry when you live there.
Those stones are yours, those noises are your mind,
The forging thunderous trams and streets that bind
You to the dreamed-of bar where sits despair
Are trams and streets: poetry is otherwise.
The cinema fronts and shops once left behind
And mourned, are mourned no more. Strangely unkind
Seem all new landmarks of the now and here.

But move you toward New Zealand or the Pole,
Those stones will blossom and the noises sing,
And trams will wheedle to the sleeping child
That never rests, whose ship will always roll,
That never can come home, but yet must bring
Strange trophies back to Ilium, and wild!

THE SHIP IS TURNING HOMEWARD

The ship is turning homeward now at last.
The bosun tries to read but dreams of home.
The old lamptrimmer sleeps, the engine thrums.
His lamps are set to light us from the past
To a near future unmysterious as this mast
With iron and what iron loves of kingdom come.
Patient iron! But, beyond the maintruck, dumb
Blankness, or the twitch of reeling stars cast
Adrift in a white ocean of doubt.
Perhaps this tramp rolls towards a futurity
That broods on ocean less than on the gall
In seamen's minds. Is that star wormwood out
Among love's stars? This freighter eternity?
Where are we going? Life save us all.

THE LIGHTHOUSE INVITES THE STORM

The lighthouse invites the storm and lights it.
Driven by tempest the tall freighter heels
Under the crag where the fiery seabird wheels,
And lightning of spume over rocks ignites it.
Oh, birds of the darkness of winter whose flights it
Importunes with frost, when ice congeals
On wings bonded for flight by zero's seals,
What good spirit undulates you still like kites that
Children are guardians of in cold blue? . . .

TASHTEGO BELIEVED RED

A hand comforts held out to one who's sinking;
And what founders deeper than a world which sinks?
Like a lost ship it never once says thanks,
Since no single hand shall save its timber drinking
The poisoned salt its sides awash are flanking,
Thirsty for web of weeds or sift of sandbanks,
Its last music gunshot, its gesture poise of tanks
Over the wood where swathes of death are ranking. . . .
But witness, the hand is no hand but an arm
Curving itself with the strong swimmer's flex
— A thousand arms which thresh against the blast
Of a regressive ocean, even whose calm
Is derelict with that impartiality which wrecks.
— Yet regard, regard, the red banner nailed to the mast!

VIGIL FORGET

Vigil Forget went ten miles on a camion,
Then a thousand or more on a freighter
Trembling in every mast; no chameleon
Changed color faster than Forget from apprehension
Of himself. His cargo of disaster grew lighter and lighter;
Once in a rickshaw he felt real condescension
Towards the present, loving it, and feeling greater
Than that ancient torturer, himself. . . . Ah, new selves!
Vigil Forget took a sampan to a far shore,
And an angry camel to Stalin's Samarkand,
And then a bleak freighter home with his poor lives
Grown self again, to board the ferry to his whore . . .
— Columbus too thought Cuba on the mainland.

THE DAYS LIKE SMITTEN CYMBALS OF BRASS

When I was young, the mildew on my soul,
like Antipholus, it chanced to me,
or Melville's Redburn, to take that soul to sea
and have it scoured.
Ah! the days like rust smitten from iron decks
were beaten into one deafening roar
of sunlight and monotony.
I had expected the roar of the sea,
and of tempest,
not this sullen unremitting calm,
this road of concrete to the Antipodes,
where thunder was gunfire behind the hull. . . .
This was not the heroic working class
where men love, looking to the future,
but petty squabbles, jealousies,
a hatred of bosuns, of Mr. Facing Both Ways,
one green eye the mate's and one the men's.
For which now's sprung for man ashore
such fierce black loathing hatred and contempt
it lives on writhing like a Kansas whirlwind
between me and these panic ports I make.
When I returned I boasted of typhoons
Conrad would not have recognized.
But to have possessed a unique anguish
has been some solace through the years.

THUNDER BEYOND
POPOCATEPETL

THUNDER BEYOND POPOCATEPETL

Black thunderclouds mass up against the wind,
High-piled beyond Popocatepetl;
So with force, against whose swollen metal
The wind of reason has the heart pinned
Till overbulged by madness, splitting mind . . .
Or, drifting without reason, see mind's petal
Torn from a good tree, but where shall it settle
But in the last darkness and at the end?
Who take no arms as the good wind's defender
You psalmists of despair, of man's approved lease,
Reason remains although your mind forsakes
It; and white birds higher fly against the thunder
Than ever flew yours, where Chekhov said was peace,
When the heart changes and the thunder breaks.

FOR *UNDER THE VOLCANO*

A dead lemon like a cowled old woman crouching in the cold.
A white pylon of salt and the flies
taxiing on the orange table, rain, rain, a scraping peon
and a scraping pen writing bowed words.
War. And the broken necked streetcars outside
and a sudden broken thought of a girl's face in Hoboken
a tilted turtle dying slowly on the stoop
of the sea-food restaurant, blood
lacing its mouth and the white floor —
ready for the ternedos tomorrow.
There will be no morrow, tomorrow is over.
Clover and the smell of fircones and the deep grass,
and turkey mole sauce and England
suddenly, a thought of home, but then
the mariachis, discordant, for the beaked bird
of maguey is on the wing, the waiter bears
a flowing black dish of emotion,
the peon's face is a mass of corruption.
We discard the horripilation of the weather
in this ghastly land of the half-buried man
where we live with Canute, the sundial and the red snapper,
the leper, the creeper, together in the green tower,
and play at sunset on the mundial flute and guitar
the song, the song of the eternal waiting of Canute,
the wrong of my waiting, the flute of my weeping,
betrothed to the puking vacuum and the unfleshible root
and the rain on the train outside creeping, creeping,

only emptiness now in my soul sleeping
where once strutted tigers lemonade scruffy green lepers
liquors pears scrubbed peppers and stuffed Leopardis;
and the sound of the train and the rain on the brain . . .
So far from barn and field and little lane —
this pyre of Bierce and springboard of Hart Crane!
Death so far away from home and wife
I fear. And prayed for my sick life —

'A corpse should be transported by express.' said the Consul
mysteriously, waking up suddenly.

XOCHITEPEC

Those animals that follow us in dream
Are swallowed by the dawn, but what of those
Which hunt us, snuff, stalk us out in life, close
In upon it, belly-down, haunt our scheme
Of building, with shapes of delirium,
Symbols of death, heraldic, and shadows,
Glowering? — Just before we left Tlalpám
Our cats lay quivering under the maguey;
A meaning had slunk, and now died, with them.
The boy slung them half stiff down the ravine,
Which now we entered, and whose name is hell.
But still our last night had its animal:
The puppy, in the cabaret, obscene,
Looping-the-loop and soiling all the floor,
And fastening itself to that horror
Of our last night: while the very last day
As I sat bowed, frozen over mescal,
They dragged two kicking fawns through the hotel
And slit their throats, behind the barroom door. . . .

The volcano is dark, and suddenly thunder
Engulfs the haciendas.
In this darkness, I think of men in the act of procreating,
Winged, stooping, kneeling, sitting down, standing up, sprawling,
Millions of trillions of billions of men moaning,
And the hand of the eternal woman flung aside.
I see their organ frozen into a gigantic rock,
Shattered now. . . .
And the cries which might be the groans of the dying
Or the groans of love —

GRIM VINEGARROON

My hate is like a wind that buffets me
All blind to need, deaf to supplication,
Scattering my words, inchoately,
Like orders shouted in a gale of wind,
The only orders that will save the ship,
Lost. From this I took refuge in your inn.
In wine recalled three good things I had done:
My last two shillings I once gave a tramp,
Which bought him but the chaos I coveted;
Succoring by death an injured scorpion;
A weeping child whose misery was mine
I gave hope to, knowing there was none.
How I congratulated my compassion!
Yet was I too that grim vinegarroon
That stings itself to death beneath the stone,
Where no message is, on the mescal plain.
So did but save myself, if not for long.
These three, against a lifetime of wrong.
What knots of self in all self-abnegation —
No other solution save the cross!

IN THE OAXACA JAIL

I have known a city of dreadful night,
Dreadfuller far than Kipling knew, or Thomson. . . .
This is the night when hope's last seed is flown
From the evanescent mind of winter's grandson.

In the dungeon shivers the alcoholic child,
Comforted by the murderer, since compassion is here too;
The noises of the night are cries for help
From the town and from the garden which evicts those who
destroy!

The policeman's shadow swings against the wall,
The lantern's shadow is darkness against the wall;
And on the cathedral's coast slowly sways the cross
— Wires and the tall pole moving in the wind —

And I crucified between two continents.

But no message whines through for me here, oh multitudinous,
To me here — (where they cure syphilis with Sloans liniment,
And clap, with another dose.)

FOR THE LOVE OF DYING

The tortures of hell are stern, their fires burn fiercely.
Yet vultures turn against the air more beautifully
than seagulls float downwind in cool sunlight,
or fans in asylums spin a loom of fate
for hope which never ventured up so high
as life's deception, astride the vulture's flight.
If death can fly, just for the love of flying,
What might not life do, for the love of dying?

DEATH OF A OAXAQUENIAN

So huge is God's despair
In the Wild cactus plain
I heard Him weeping there

That I might venture where
The peon had been slain
So huge is God's despair

On the polluted air
Twixt noonday and the rain
I heard Him weeping there

And felt His anguish tear
For refuge in my brain
So huge is God's despair

That it could find a lair
In one so small and vain
I heard Him weeping there

Oh vaster than our share
Than deserts of new Spain
So huge is God's despair
I heard Him weeping there. . . .

IN A MEXICAN CHURCH

Christ, slashed with an axe, in the humped church —
How shall we pray to you all pied with blood,
Yet deader by far than the hacked wood?
But pray we must since prayer is all our search
Who come in anger only to beseech.
Here kneel two creatures who believe in good,
Here stood two lovers, they believed in God,
And in thee, too, though maimed at life's touch
As by the doleful art of these dull men.
— Oh, ravaged by man but murdered in mankind.
Of peace a prater, yet of fire and shot
Vicarious exculpator to seventy times seven;
Image, we wish thee ill; yet alive in mind
That mind itself may live, and compassion forsake us not.

DELIRIUM IN VERA CRUZ

Where has tenderness gone, he asked the mirror
Of the Baltimore Hotel, cuarto 216. Alas,
Can its reflection lean against the glass
Too, wondering where I have gone, into what horror?
Is that it staring at me now with terror
Behind your frail tilted barrier? Tenderness
Was here, in this very bedroom, in this
Place, its form seen, cries heard, by you. What error
Is here? Am I that rashed image?
Is this the ghost of the love you reflected?
Now with a background of tequila, stubs, dirty collars,
Sodium perborate, and a scrawled page
To the dead, telephone off the hook? In rage
He smashed all the glass in the room. (Bill: $50.)

SUNRISE

Sober I rode into the bran new dawn,
With steady hand grasping the single rein,
New-shod new-shrived and all but newly born
Over the smiling grandiloquent plain.

Surcingleless as heaven ran my steed
And true to heaven rose my simple song,
Ah, the years behind seemed lost, and lost the deed,
As pommel and stirrups unheeded I cantered along.

— But what cactuses are these on every hand,
Wild dogs and spectres, all enveloping?
And came again into that evening land,

Galloping, galloping, galloping —

Bound to that unrelenting fatuous horse
Whose eyes are lidless and whose name, remorse.

THE CANTINAS

PRAYER FOR DRUNKS

God give those drunkards drink who wake at dawn
Gibbering on Beelzebub's bosom, all outworn,
As once more through the windows they espy
Looming, the dreadful Pontefract of day.

THIRTY-FIVE MESCALS IN CUAUTLA

This ticking is most terrible of all —
You hear the sound I mean on ships and trains.
You hear it everywhere. for it is doom;
the tick of real death, not the tick of time;
the termite at the rotten wainscot of the world —
And it is death to you, though well you know
The heart's silent tick failing against the clock,
Its beat ubiquitous and still more slow:
But still not the tick, the tick of real death,
Only the tick of time — still only the heart's chime
When body's alarm wakes whirring to terror.

In the cantina throbs the refrigerator,
While against the street the gaunt station hums.
What can you say fairly of a broad lieutenant,
With bloody hand behind him, a cigarro in it,
But that he blocks a square of broken sunlight
Where scraps of freedom stream against the gale
And lightning scrapes blue shovels against coal?
The thunder batters the Gothic mountains;
But why must you hear, hear and not know this storm.
Seeing it only under the door,
Visible in synecdoches of wheels
And khaki water sousing down the gutter?
In ripples like claws tearing the water back?
The wheels smash a wake under the jalousie.

The lieutenant moves, but the door swings to. . . .
What of all this life outside, unseen by you,
Passed by, escaped from, or excluded
By a posture in a desolate bar? . . . .
No need to speak, conserve a last mistake;
Perhaps real death's inside, don't let it loose.
The lieutenant carried it into the back room?
The upturned spittoons may mean it, so may the glass.
The girl refills it, pours a glass of death,
And if that death's in her it's here in me.
On the pictured calendar, set to the future,
The two reindeer battle to death, while man,
The tick of real death, not the tick of time,
Hearing, thrusts his canoe into a moon,*
Risen to bring us madness none too soon.
(1937)

*Author's note: Soma was mystically identified with the moon, who controls vegetation, and whose cup is ever filling and emptying, as he waxes and wanes.

EYE-OPENER

How like a man, is Man, who rises late
And gazes on his unwashed dinner plate
And gazes on the bottles, empty too,
Ali gulphed in last night's loud long how-do-you-do,
— Although one glass yet holds a gruesome bait —
How like to Man is this man and his fate,
Still drunk and stumbling through the rusty trees
To breakfast on stale rum sardines and peas.

NO COMPANY BUT FEAR

How did all this begin and why am I here
at this arc of bar with its cracked brown paint,
papegaai, mezcal, hennessey, cerveza,
two slimed spittoons, no company but fear:
fear of light, of the spring, of the complaint
of birds and buses flying to far places,
and the students going to the races,
of girls skipping with the wind in their faces,
but no company, no company but fear,
fear of the blowing fountain: and all flowers
that know the sun are my enemies,
these, dead, hours?

NO TIME TO STOP AND THINK

The only hope is the next drink.
If you like, you take a walk.
No time to stop and think,
The only hope is the next drink.
Useless trembling on the brink,
Worse than useless all this talk.
The only hope is the next drink.
If you like, *you* take a walk.

COMFORT

You are not the first man to have the shakes,
the wheels, the horrors, to wear the scarlet
snowshoe, nor yet the invincible harlot
dogged by eyes like fishnets. Leaning, aches
the iron face with agate eyes, and wakes
the guardian angel, sees the past
a parthenon of possibilities. . . .
You are not the first man to be caught lying,
nor to be told that you are dying.

WITHOUT THE NIGHTED WYVERN

Notions of freedom are tied up with drink.
Our ideal life contains a tavern
Where man may sit and talk or just think,
All without fear of the nighted wyvern;
Or yet another tavern where it appears
There are no No Trust signs no No Credit
And, apart from the unlimited beers,
We sit unhackled drunk and mad to edit
Tracts of a really better land where man
May drink a finer, ah, an undistilled wine
That subtly intoxicates without pain,
Weaving the vision of the unassimilable inn
Where we may drink forever without owing
With the door open, and the wind blowing.

THE DRUNKARDS

The noise of death is in this desolate bar,
Where tranquility sits bowed over its prayer
And music shells the dream of the lover,
But when no nickel brings this harsh despair
Into this loneliest of homes
And of all dooms the loneliest yet,
When no electric music breaks the beat
Of hearts to be doubly broken but now set
By the surgeon of peace in the splint of woe,
Pierces more deeply than trumpets do
The motion of the mind into that web
Where disorders are as simple as the tomb
And the spider of life sits, sleep.

AT THE BAR

— Drunkards of salt water, thirsty for disaster,
Derelicts do not dream of being ships:
Never does calamity forsake them
For the hush of the swift and the look-out's all's well:
Neurotic in Atlantic of a death,
Bereaved but avid of another's breath,
Swimming with black genius under black waters,
And buried standing up like Ben Johnson,
Though eighteenpence is here a total loss;
And Tarquin certain of a ravishable prey;
While others grope the rails, rigid with gazing down.

SESTINA IN A CANTINA

Scene: A waterfront tavern in Vera Cruz at daybreak.

LEGION
Watching this dawn's mnemonic of old dawning:
Jonquil-colored, delicate, some in prison,
Green dawns of drinking tenderer than sunset,
But clean and delicate like dawns of ocean
Flooding the heart with pale light in which horrors
Stampede like plump wolves in distorting mirrors.

Oh, we have seen ourselves in many mirrors;
Confusing all our sunsets with the dawning,
Investing every tongue and leaf with horrors,
And every stranger overtones for prison,
And seeing mainly in the nauseous ocean
The last shot of our life before the sunset.

ST. LUKE (a ship's doctor)
How long since you have really seen a sunset?
The mind has many slanting lying mirrors,
The mind is like that sparkling greenhouse ocean
Glass-deceptive in the Bengal dawning;
The mind has ways of keeping us in prison,
The better there to supervise its horrors.

SIR PHILIP SIDNEY

Why do you not, sir, organize your horrors
And shoot them one day, preferably at sunset,

That we may wake up next day not in prison,
No more deceived by lies and many mirrors,
And go down to the cold beach at dawning
To lave away the past in colder ocean?

ST. LUKE

No longer is there freedom on the ocean.
And even if there were, he likes his horrors,
And if he shot them would do so at dawning
That he might have acquired some more by sunset,
Breaking them in by that time before mirrors
To thoughts of spending many nights in prison.

LEGION

The fungus-colored sky of dawns in prison,
The fate that broods on every pictured ocean,
The fatal conversations before mirrors,
The fiends and all the spindly breeds of horrors,
Have shattered by their beauty every sunset
And rendered quite intolerable old dawning.

The oxen standing motionless at dawning —
Outside our tavern now, outside our prison —
Red through the wagon wheels. jalousies like sunset,

Swinging now in a sky as calm as ocean,
Where Venus hangs her obscene horn of horrors
For us now swaying in a hall of mirrors —

Such horrid beauty maddened all my mirrors,
Has burst in heart's eye sanity of dawning,
No chamber in my house brimful of horrors
But does not whisper of some dreadful prison,
Worse than all ships dithering through the ocean
Tottering like drunkards, arms upraised at sunset.

RICHARD III (a barman)
Vain derelict all avid for the sunset!
Shine out fair sun till you have bought new mirrors
That you may see your shadow pass the ocean,
And sunken no more pass our way at dawning,
But lie on the cold stone sea floor of some prison,
A chunk of sodden driftwood gnawed by horrors.

LEGION
At first I never looked on them as horrors;
But one day I was drinking hard near sunset,
And suddenly saw the world as a giant prison,
Ruled by tossing moose-heads, with hand mirrors,
And heard the voice of the idiot speak at dawning,
And since that time have dwelt beside the ocean.

EL UNIVERSAL (early edition)
Did no one speak of love beside the ocean,
Have you not felt, even among your horrors,
Granting them, there was such a thing as dawning,
A dawning for man whose star seems now at sunset,
Like million-sheeted scarlet dusty mirrors,
But one day must be led out of his prison?

LEGION
I see myself as all mankind in prison,
With hands outstretched to lanterns by the ocean;
I see myself as all mankind in mirrors,
Babbling of love while at his back rise horrors
Ready to suck the blood out of the sunset
And amputate the godhead of the dawning.

THE SWINE
And now the dawning drives us from our prison
Into the dawn like sunset, into the ocean,
Bereaving him of horrors, but leaving him his mirrors. . . .

VENUS

VENUS

And, when you go — much as a meteor,
Or as this swaying, incandescent car,
Which, like lost love, leaves lightnings in its wake,
(And me, an aspen with its Christ in mind,
Whose wood remembers once it made a cross,
So trembles ever since in wind, or no wind)
But most like Venus, with our black desire
Which blinds me now, your light a horned curve
First; then, circling, a whitely flaming disc,
Not distance, but your phase, removes the mask —
Until you burn the brightest of all stars —
Pray then in your most brilliant lonely hour
That, reunited, we may learn forever
To keep the sun between ourselves and love.

FRAGMENT

A wounded voice over the telephone:
"Call me later. I am just tired."
— Then, the bell shrieking in the unseen room
Filling it with the ferocity of doom.
"But what shall I do, my own, my lost one,
Latched back into deeper night from the dark's drone?
They have called back the last, the slowest of all
                              to the asylum,

Whose only thought is time, now there is none,
Now all is gone, all, all, save compassion,
And all is doubly gone with you gone, dear."
— The bell still beats about that tragic room
Like a trapped bird, precurrer of greater fear,
Where I imagine every book we shared,
Touched, yes, touched, smell, out of the pages of a book,
Out of Gogol; or your heart fluttering in my hand
That once drew notes of love from your flesh's viol
But never held your heart back from denial,
Nor teeth, from my own heartsneck. . . .
— The stars like silver rifles in the void
Look down their sights to their special aim.
They do not range the categories of our pain. . . .
No world will plunge for tears we never saw fall,
For sorrow that was never shared at all,
That I might comfort the dead, clasp stones in the stream.

A NEW SHIP

Like the black iron steps
leading from some aerial footway
flung over road and lines down at the dockside
crowded with holiday makers
is the past ——

and evermore my mind climbs down that stair
to find, below, the selfsame wharf, despair.

But one day a new ship is waiting there.

A POEM OF GOD'S MERCY

Cain shall not slay Abel today on our good ground,
Nor Adam reel under our shrouded moon,
Nor Ishmael lie stiff in 28th Street,
With a New Bedford harpoon in his brain,
His right lung in a Hoboken garboon.
For this is the long day when the lost are found,
And those, parted by tragedy, meet
With spring-sweet joy. And those who longest should have met
Are safe in each other's arms not too late.
Today the forsaken one of the fold is brought home,
And the great cold, in the street of the vulture, are warm,
The numbed albatross is sheltered from the storm,
The tortured shall no longer know alarm,
For all in wilderness are free from harm:
Age dreaming on youth, youth dreaming on age, shall not be
                                                    found,

While good Loki chases dragons underground.
Life hears our prayer for the lonely trimmer on watch,
Or shuddering, at one bell, on the wet hatch
At evening, for the floating sailor by the far coast,
The impaled soldier in the shell-hole or the hail,
The crew of the doomed barque sweeping into the sunset
With black sails; for mothers in anguish and unrest,
And for each of all the damned and the oppressed,
Will recommence the Pentecost.

Ah, poets of God's mercy, harbingers of the gale,
Now I say the lamb is brought home, and Gogol
Wraps a warm overcoat about him. . . .
Our city of dreadful night will blossom into a sea-morning!
Only bear with us, bear with my song,
For at dawn is the reckoning. And this last night is long.

A QUARREL

The poignance of a quarrel in the post!
That threat, flung at myself into a pillar,
Which could have been as a white bird loosed
Homing, with news of reprieve, to your heart —
Would that the tyrannous thing might be lost,
Sorted into the dark, by some eerie scrivener. . . .
The wind is high to-night in Canada,
A viaduct is drifting out to sea,
Ground lightning felled a tree across the street,
And direst portent's here for all save me.
For still the wheels cry out against the iron,
And frozen platforms race back into day.
Ah, that I could believe, when wires are down,
That venom such as mine could lose its way.

NO STILL PATH

Alas, there is no still path in my soul,
I being evil, none of memory;
No path, untenanted by friend or ghoul,
Where those I have loved best touch wings and sigh
And passing enter silently the place
Of dream, illumined by bright fruit, and light,
That circles from the always brightest face
Of love itself, and dissipates the night.
There is no path, there is no path at all,
Unless perhaps where abstract things have gone
And precepts rise and metaphysics fall,
And principles abandoned stumble on.
No path, but as it were a river in spate
Where drowning forms, downswept, gesticulate.

NOCTURNE

This evening Venus sings alone
And homeward feathers stir like silk
Like the dress of a multitudinous ghost
The pinions tear through a sky like milk.
Seagulls all soon to be turned to stone
That seeking I lose beyond the trail
In the woods that I and my ignorance own
Where together we walk on our hands and knees
Together go walking beneath the pale
Of a beautiful evening loved the most
And yet this evening is my jail
And policemen glisten in the trees.

SAINT MALCOLM AMONG THE BIRDS

And now the seagulls peck on the front porch:
Waxwings, circling the roof, precisely drop:
Even the kingfisher rests from debauch
Contemplating me from a salt grey prop
That can look after itself; with kinship's eye
Thus I have humbled myself for birds only.
A veritable St. Francis — was it? — I
But lick the sores of my own leprosy.
A certain stingy adulation steams
From all this noble cloying behaviour
Nor would I put past my ego's schemes
To identify myself as some white saviour —
Were not this retreat to love from stalemate
Merely the rearguard action of my hate.

HAPPINESS

Blue mountains with snow and blue cold rough water,
A wild sky full of stars at rising
And Venus and the gibbous moon at sunrise,
Gulls following a motorboat against the wind,
Trees with branches rooted in air —
Sitting in the sun at noon with the furiously
Smoking shadow of the shack chimney —
Eagles drive downwind in one,
Terns blow backward,
A new kind of tobacco at eleven,
And my love returning on the four o'clock bus
— My God, why have you given this to us?

BE PATIENT FOR THE WOLF

Be patient for the wolf is always with you.
Listen, little idiot, for the sound of your desire;
Do not be deceived it is not the sea,
The wolf is madness but the moon is light.
God will come out of such ignorance as this,
Not like a jack-in-the-box but like a tree
Turned weeping father in delirium.
The woes of night all have their tragic place,
Half the face of God seeks half its face.
And He will find your genius in the dark
And give it back without a bondsman.

Be patient for the wolf is ever with you,
Ugly and wicked one and yet divine.
Forget the shrieking of the sea
The contemptuous sea curling its lip all day,
Strident as factories of shattering glass.
Pass by the sleek unvintageable sea
For those who drink her deepest are the drowned.
The black snow is piled high under the clock
Where broken tryst meets broken heart in time.
This is a world of worthless mysteries.
Be patient for much much much is patient.

Be patient for the wolf is patient,
Whose small shadow has stopped here.
The meadows wait for rainbows to say God,

The shadows wait for you to say the word,
Two pillows look to love to save the world.
The moonlit collier reels at a foul anchor.
The charter waits: the ship freezes in the fjord.
The angel waits: his heart an aching hand
To win you from us to the evening land
Where no one ravens but where things are made,
And where no wolf is nor no thought of flood.

Be patient because the wolf is patient.
The redbreast waits for redress from the dark,
The swallow pines for autumn to say now,
And Echo, for Hero not to reply no.
Only the bell that follows does not wait
Galloping mother-faced across the fields
To abrase you to the bone with a rough chime.
At the beginning of the inferno, in the middle
Of the wood, the image teeters between mother and sea.
Pay no heed to the bell nor to the aged sea
But to the dear kind wolf pay allegiance.

Be patient, because of the wolf, be patient:
The squeaks and woes of night all have their place.
You'll find your blood-warm cave and rest at last;
The shadows wait for you to say the word.
Listen now to your own soft cunning step.
Be patient, because of the wolf be patient-
His step is your own now, you are free, being bereft.

THE COMEDIAN

THE COMEDIAN

He plays the piano with a razor,
The concertina with a pair of scissors;
A rigadoon for all his customers,
He is the Sweeny Tod of improvisors!
Though all men fear this poor relation,
His keener music gives a strange sensation;
Defying all anatomization,
Beckoning like ambiguous sounds,
Heard by those who dwelt with Cyclops and fiends,
And died on perfumed seas with stinking wounds. . . .
Under the razor, under the broken light
Of this gibbering world we shall fall
Thus enticed, into the swinging chair to wait;
Read madness: watch self; accept nothing; accept all.

MEN WITH COATS THRASHING

Our lives we do not weep
Are like wild cigarettes
That on a stormy day
Men light against the wind
With cupped and practised hand
Then burn themselves as deep
As debts we cannot pay
And smoke themselves so fast
One scarce gives time to light
A second life that might
Flake smoother than the first
And have no taste at last
And most are thrown away.

THOUGHTS WHILE DROWNING

Let others quarrel above my grief
raven like wolves over a cache of meat
my grief is now the property of the state
long self-starved it is on relief
many of these with surfeit of happiness need it

the evening darkens with a sense of guilt
like a thunderstorm blackening the promontory
smearing the remembered headland of a life
with a child's scrawl of chaos against the night
the tourists wait with fatuous smiles of triumph
with bereaved arms upon the gossiping shore
having known the corpse they are for a moment great.

QUEER POEM

I knew a man without a heart:
Boys tore it out, they said,
And gave it to a hungry wolf
Who picked it up and fled.

And fled the boys, their master too,
All distant fled the brute,
And after it, in quaint pursuit,
The heartless man reeled on.

I met this man the other day
Walking in grotesque pride.
His heart restored, his mien gay,
The meek wolf by his side.

POEM

Wet streets in Liverpool
Wet streets in Hartlepool
And frightful viaducts at night
Whence are seen strange pillars of light
Weep for me.

MIDTOWN PYROMANIAC

The midtown pyromaniac, sunset,
Has set fire to all the aerieled roofs,
And you and I, talking, wait the onset
Of the last night, meek as eight standing hooves,
Or penned plump beeves loved not beyond slaughter.
Here is a thought — read when the journey palls —
Nor turn from corridor trees or laughter:
The horror is, the curtain never falls
On the dull interminable murder,
Nor will eyes rest in death's democracy;
Delirium's there, and there the girder
Is set, the house raised to hypocrisy.
Good bye, old comrade, of your death I pray
It prove sweet marjoram nor turn caraway.

INJURED STONES

A child may find no words for its sorrow
But may hear at nightfall strange presage of release
That injured stones know pressing to the earth,
Or he may learn that stones themselves may speak
Flintly their language of heartbreak.
In the cloakroom is the roar of the sea
And a rebuke, but even that is comfort
In that it means one less rebuke
Between himself and death. . . .
And on the hearthrug gazing into hell
There is the future — the stokehold perhaps —
Yet I think there must have been laughter,
The sole recovery, men say, from life,
And had he not survived it
Would he have known that Rimbaud felt the same,
Whose manhood was as loveless and as dumb?

EPITAPH

Malcolm Lowry
Late of the Bowery
His prose was flowery
And often glowery
He lived, nightly, and drank, daily,
And died playing the ukulele.

SONGS FROM

THE BEACH: ERIDANUS

KINGFISHERS IN BRITISH COLUMBIA

A mad kingfisher
rocketing about in the
red fog at sunrise

now sits
on the alder
post that tethers the floats
angrily awaiting his mate.
Here she

comes, like a left wing
three quarter cutting through toward
the goal in sun-lamped
fog at Rosslyn Park at half
past three in halcyon days.

CHRIST WALKS IN THIS INFERNAL DISTRICT TOO

Beneath the Malebolge lies Hastings Street,
The province of the pimp upon his beat,
Where each in his little world of drugs or crime
Moves helplessly or, hopeful, begs a dime
Wherewith to purchase half a pint of piss —
Although he will be cheated, even in this.
I hope, although I doubt it, God knows
This place where chancres blossom like the rose,
For on each face is such a hard despair
That nothing like a grief could enter there.
And on this scene from all excuse exempt
The mountains gaze in absolute contempt,
Yet this is also Canada, my friend,
Yours to absolve of ruin, or make an end.

WHIRLPOOL

Resurgent sorrow is a sea in the cave
Of the mind — just as in the poem
It gluts it — though no nymphs will quire a hymn;
Abandon it! . . . Take a trip to the upper shore. Lave
Yourself in sand; gather poppies; brave
The fringe of things, denying that inner chasm.
Why, the hush of the sea's in the seashell; in the limb
Of the smashed ship, its tempest; and your grave
The sand itself if you'd have it so. Yet glare
Through a sky of love all day, still must you receive
In that cave the special anguish of your life;
With the skull of the seagull and the wreck you may fare
Well enough, but will not escape the other surf,
Remorse, your host, who haunts the whirlpool where
The past's not washed up dead and black and dry
But whirls in its gulf forever, to no relief.

HOSTAGE

A day of sunlight and swallows . . .
And saw the fireman, by the fiddley, wave.
And laughed. And went on digging my own grave.

THE GLAUCOUS-WINGED GULL

The hook-nosed angel that walks like a sailor,
Pure scavenger of the empyrean,
Hunter of edible stars, and sage
Catsbane and defiler of the porch,
Dead sailor, finial, and image
Of freedom in morning blue, and strange torch
At twilight, stranger world of love,
Old haunter of the Mauretania,
Snowblinded once, I saved. And hove
Out of the rainbarrel, back at heaven —
A memory stronger than childhood's even
Or freighters rolling to Roumania.

THE SHIP SAILS ON:
FOR NORDAHL GRIEG

Now we have considered these things, each to each,
The house in the marsh like home; the factories
With torn smoke evanescent as farewell;
The swift ship, and solitary landward gull;
And with its special currents, the river,
(Which throws a sudden wash upon the beach),
Negotiable as a simple poem; trees,
Nameless, but friendly sentinels; and nowhere
Pandemonium of our enemies, —
The news of how one fought, another fell,
To conjure up such landscape with his blood,
Shakes us with an anguished, secret laughter,
Since all we know is that the wind is good,
And at the end the sun is what it was.

THE WOUNDED BAT

. . . on a summer's afternoon, hot
and in the dusty path a bat,
with injured membrane and little hands,
a meeting that would have knocked young Aeschylus flat,
its red mouth helpless, like a mouse or cat,
a buzzing, like a buzzer, electric,
pathetic crepitation in the path.
She hooked to the twig, I laid her in the shade
with compassion, yet with blind terror
praying that not too soon
death might care to do for me as much.

THE PAST

Like a rotten old ladder
cast adrift from a dismantled sawmill
to float, shoulders awash, the rest
waterlogged, eaten by teredos,
barnacle encrusted, shellfish
clinging in blue gravelottes,
stinking, heavy with weeds, the strange life
of death and low tide, vermiculated,
helminthiatic,
seems my conscience —
hauled out now to dry in the sun,
leaning against nothing,
leading nowhere —
but to be put to use perhaps,
salvageable — to be graved,
up and down which
each night my
mind meaninglessly
climbs.

THE PILGRIM

A pilgrim passes through the town by night,
An ignorant, an insignificant man.
He was a pilgrim when the world began
To read strange huntsmen in the infinite.
The cliffs are on the left, while to the right
The sea is like the sea whose rumour ran
Once in his childhood through the thundery plain.
The sea was hope then, and the rumour bright.
The cliffs are high, the sea is far too deep,
The town is just a lie, twitching with lies.
— Would that I had the courage not to sleep,
I may not follow, when may I arise?
Teach me to navigate the fjords of chance
Winding through my abyssal ignorance.

THE WILD CHERRY

We put a prop beneath the sagging bough
That yearned over the beach, setting four stones
Cairn-like against it, but we thought our groans
Were the wild cherry's, for it was as though,
Utterly set with broken seams on doom,
It listed wilfully down like a mast,
Stubborn as some smashed recalcitrant boom
That will neither be cut loose nor made fast.
Going — going — it was yet no bidder
For life, whether for such sober healing
We left its dead branches to consider
Until its sunward pulse renewed, feeling
The passionate hatred of that tree
Whose longing was to wash away to sea.

THE LANGUAGE
OF MAN'S WOE

RILKE AND YEATS

Help me to write.
Show me the gates
Where the orders are,
And the cage
My soul stares at,
Where my courage
Roars through the grates.

THOUGHTS TO BE ERASED FROM MY DESTINY

He reads and reads, this poet to be,
Perhaps in this very anthology —

Revised that is, ten years from now,
Which gives our poet ample time to grow —

He reads and reads, but does not understand,
Set at a tangent even in his own land;

Reads more as if writing between their lines,
In which scant sense or fury he divines.

To their aggregate daemon
His forces stand as firemen to seamen.

He reads but does not understand,

Save where, in some fragment of biography,
Is written: "Perished by his own hand."

JOSEPH CONRAD

This wrestling, as of seamen with a storm
Which flies to leeward — while they, united
In that chaos, turn, each on his nighted
Bunk, to dream of chaos again, or home —
The poet himself, struggling with the form
Of his coiled work, knows; having requited
Sea-weariness with purpose, invited
What derricks of the soul plunge in his room.
Yet some mariner's ferment in his blood
— Though truant heart will hear the iron travail
And song of ships that ride their easting down —
Sustains him to subdue or be subdued.
In sleep all night he grapples with a sail!
But words beyond the life of ships dream on.

TRINITY

Imprisoned in a Liverpool of self
I haunt the gutted arcades of the past.
Where it lies on some high forgotten shelf
I find what I was looking for at last.
But now the shelf has turned into a mast
And now the mast into an uptorn tree
Where one sways crucified twixt two of me.

THE DOOMED IN THEIR SINKING

We likened one man to a ship adrift,
Broken from anchorage with skeleton crew
Of false precepts; or listing with iceberg's impact.
It was melancholy to hear him try to shift
The blame on us for his sure guilt; but gift
Of clarity he lacked, and in fact,
No tactile appeal for help was made anew;
It was long before he was silent. I tried to sift
Later the mystery of man's dissembling
When most he needs aid. We would have
Given him that. . . . I have considered it since.
When the doomed are most eloquent in their sinking,
It seems that then we are least strong to save,
And pray that his prove no titanic case.

EELS

Eels seem to spawn in the deep dark water:
Nobody has seen them apparently;
No one has seen their eggs, only later
The larva rise, knife-like, transparently.
Open sea young eels turn into glass eels
Moving only by day to the far shores.
But nobody knows it, nobody reels
Them in as they breast even Niagaras.
Then they swim back by night to their great grave
In the abysses of the Hebrides.
Their shape is like their life and like the wave
That breaks over them is the death of these.
The will of the eel is its destiny.
No eel ever comes back from that dark sea.

THE PLAGIARIST (fragment)

. . . See the wound the upturned stone has left
In the earth! How doubly tragic is the hollowed shape —
It is a miracle that I may use such words
As shape. But the analogy has escaped.
Crawling on hands and sinews to the grave
I found certain pamphlets on the way.
Said they were mine. For they explained a pilgrimage
That otherwise was meaningless as day
But twice as difficult, to explain away. . . .

HE LIKED THE DEAD

As the poor end of each dead day drew near
he tried to count the things which he held dear.
No Rupert Brooke and no great lover, he
remembered little of simplicity:
his soul had never been empty of fear
and he would sell it thrice now for a tarot of beer.
He seemed to have known no love, to have valued dread
above all human feelings. He liked the dead.
The grass was not green not even grass to him;
nor was sun, sun; rose, rose; smoke, smoke; limb, limb.

AFTER PUBLICATION OF UNDER *THE VOLCANO*

Success is like some horrible disaster
Worse than your house burning, the sounds of ruination
As the roof tree falls following each other faster
While you stand, the helpless witness of your damnation.

Fame like a drunkard consumes the house of the soul
Exposing that you have worked for only this —
Ah, that I had never suffered this treacherous kiss
And had been left in darkness forever to founder and fail.

THE SEARCH

In Dante no, in Shakespeare no,
Nor yet in any library you go.
And in His book you scarcely dare
To hope you'll find your agony there.

STRANGE TYPE

I wrote: in the dark cavern of our birth.
The printer had it tavern, which seems better:
But herein lies the subject of our mirth,
Since on the next page death appears as dearth.
So it may be that God's word was distraction,
Which to our strange type appears destruction,
Which is bitter.

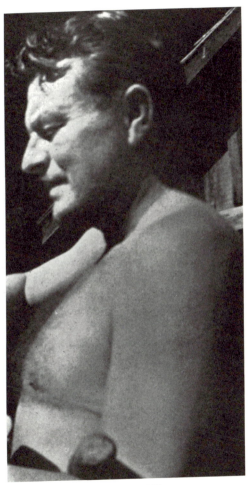

Dollarton, 1952.

Dollarton, Summer 1953.

The Lake District, England, June 1957.

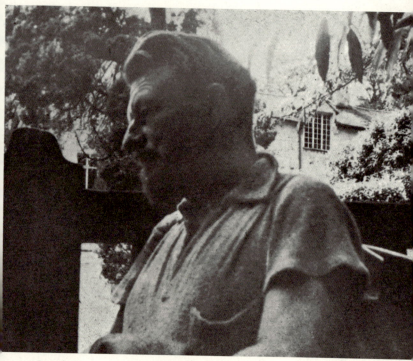

Outside Wordsworth's house, The Lake District, England, 1957. (Last photo of Lowry)